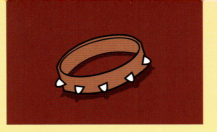

EYE TO EYE WITH DOGS

DALMATIANS

Lynn M. Stone

Rourke
Publishing LLC
Vero Beach, Florida 32964

© 2005 Rourke Publishing LLC

All rights reserved. No part of this book may be reproduced or utilized in any form or by any means, electronic or mechanical including photocopying, recording, or by any information storage and retrieval system without permission in writing from the publisher.

www.rourkepublishing.com

PHOTO CREDITS: All photos © Lynn M. Stone

Title page: *Dalmatian pups end playtime with a group nap.*

Acknowledgments: For their help in the preparation of this book, the author thanks Lynette Blackman, Mike and Maureen Deer, and Phillip Kroovand.

Editor: Frank Sloan

Cover and page design by Nicola Stratford

Library of Congress Cataloging-in-Publication Data

Stone, Lynn M.
 Dalmatians / Lynn M. Stone.
     p. cm. -- (Eye to eye with dogs II)
 Includes bibliographical references and index.
    ISBN 1-59515-160-5 (hardcover)
 1. Dalmatian dog--Juvenile literature. I. Title. II. Series: Stone, Lynn M. Eye to eye with dogs II.
 SF429.D3S76 2004
 636.72--dc22

2004008025

Printed in the USA

CG/CG

Table of Contents

The Dalmatian	5
The Dog for You?	11
Dalmatians of the Past	17
Looks	20
A Note about Dogs	22
Glossary	23
Index	24
Further Reading/Website	24

The Dalmatian wears a flashy coat of white with black or dark brown spots.

The Dalmatian

It would be hard to mistake the handsome Dalmatian for any other dog. It is the only dog **breed** with spots! It may also be the only dog with such a long list of **accomplishments**.

The Dalmatian has been a bird and rat hunter, a carriage dog, a firehouse dog, and a rescue dog. It has been a retriever, herder of cattle and sheep, a circus dog, and even the star of a book and two films. Today it is mostly a lovable household companion.

DALMATIAN FACTS

Weight: 40-60 pounds (18-27 kilograms)
Height: 19-23 inches (49-59 centimeters)
Country of Origin: India?
Life Span: 12-14 years

In the late 1800s and early 1900s Dalmatians were best known for working with horses. In England the **stylish** Dalmatians tirelessly trotted along with horse-drawn carriages.

Dalmatians make loving pets.

Dalmatians like to retrieve objects.

The dogs protected the horses from roaming dogs and seemed to calm the horses. When the carriages stopped for the night, the dogs guarded against horse thieves.

Between 1870 and 1910, especially in the United States, Dalmatians were **mascots** for horse-drawn fire wagons. When automobiles and trucks replaced carriages and fire wagons, Dalmatians lost some of their popularity. A few firehouses, however, still keep Dalmatian mascots.

A Dalmatian perches on the bumper of a fire engine.

A few Dalmatians can still be seen at firehouses.

British author Dodie Smith helped bring the Dalmatian's popularity back with her book *101 Dalmatians* in 1956. Two Disney movies by the same title, in 1961 and 1996, also gave Dalmatians a boost in popularity.

Dalmatian pups were the stars of 10l Dalmatians.

An affectionate Dalmatian bounds into its owner's arms.

The Dog for You?

Dalmatians are affectionate dogs, at least to the people they know. Because Dalmatians are not friendly to strangers, they make good watchdogs. And they are big and strong enough to make reasonably good guard dogs.

A Dalmatian's short coat makes it more of a summer dog than a winter dog. But the short coat is easy to groom.

Dalmatians may be kept indoors or outdoors, depending on the weather. However, Dalmatians need a great deal of human attention, and they are best cared for living indoors.

Dalmatians love the outdoors.

Because they are athletic, Dalmatians love to romp.

At the same time, Dalmatians are highly **energetic** and athletic. They love to run and, given the chance, they'll roam.

Dalmatians need plenty of hard exercise time. They need more than a quick walk on a leash. Dalmatians need active owners who will run or jog with them and toss a Frisbee from time to time.

Dalmatians love hard play, like a Frisbee toss.

On a long morning walk, a Dalmatian doubles its spots in the mirror of a woodland pool.

Dalmatians of the Past

Dalmatians have been known in Europe since the 1500s. But where the breed began and how it got its spots is a mystery. Some evidence suggests that Dalmatians began in India and were brought to Europe by traders. What Dalmatians were first **bred** to do is also a mystery.

The Dalmatian is named for Dalmatia, a part of Croatia on the Adriatic Sea. It is unlikely, though, that the breed actually began there.

Where the Dalmatian's spots came from is unknown.

A Dalmatian's body build and long, whiplike tail are similar to a pointer's.

Among the Dalmatian's **ancestors** may have been the pointer and a small, spotted Great Dane. Dalmatians and pointers certainly share a similar shape.

Looks

All Dalmatians look like they have been standing under a dripping paint bucket. But some, of course, have far more spots than others. The spots may be black or liver, a dark brown color.

This Dalmatian has liver-colored spots.

Dalmatians, like this one, often have one blue eye and one brown eye.

The dog has floppy ears, a deep chest, and a long, whiplike tail on a medium-sized body. Its eyes may be brown, gold, or blue.

Dalmatian pups are born white. Their spots begin to show in two to three weeks.

A Note about Dogs

Puppies are cute and cuddly, but only after serious thought should anybody buy one. Puppies grow up.

And remember that a dog will require more than love and patience. It will need healthy food, exercise, grooming, a warm, safe place in which to live, and medical care.

A dog can be your best friend, but you need to be its best friend, too.

Choosing the right breed requires some homework. For more information about buying and owning a dog, contact the American Kennel Club at http://www.akc.org/index.cfm or the Canadian Kennel Club at http://www.ckc.ca/.

Glossary

accomplishment (uh KOM plish munt) — a personal success; that which has been done well

ancestor (AN SES tur) — an animal that at some past time was part of the modern animal's family

bred (BRED) — to have been born to do a certain thing

breed (BREED) — a particular kind of domestic animal within a larger, closely related group, such as the Dalmatian breed within the dog group

energetic (EN ur JET ik) — to be full of energy, high spirits

mascot (MAS kut) — a companion chosen as a good luck symbol

stylish (STY lish) — to show handsome or flashy good looks

Index

ancestors 19	horses 6, 7
carriages 6, 7, 8	India 17
coat 11	mascots 8
Dalmatia 18	pointer 20
Europe 17	Smith, Dodie 9
eyes 21	spots 5, 17, 20, 21
fire wagons 8	tail 21
guard dogs 11	watchdogs 11

Further Reading

Carroll, David L. *The ASPCA Complete Guide to Pet Care.* Plume, 2001
Fogle, Bruce. *The Dog Owner's Manual.* DK Publishing, 2003
Quasha, Jennifer. *Story of the Dalmatian.* Rosen, 2003
Wilcox, Charlotte. *Dalmatian.* Capstone, 1996

Websites to Visit

Dalmatian Club of America at www.thedca.org

About the Author

Lynn M. Stone is the author of more than 400 children's books. He is a talented natural history photographer as well. Lynn, a former teacher, travels worldwide to photograph wildlife in its natural habitat.